T0023811

THINK
LITTLE

Think Little

ESSAYS

Wendell Berry

COUNTERPOINT
Berkeley, California

THINK LITTLE

"Think Little" first appeared in *A Continuous
Harmony: Essays Cultural and Agricultural*. "A Native
Hill" first appeared in *The Long-Legged House*.

ISBN: 978-1-64009-173-3

The Library of Congress Cataloging-in-Publication
Data is available.

Cover design by Jenny Carrow
Book design by Jordan Koluch

COUNTERPOINT
2560 Ninth Street, Suite 318
Berkeley, CA 94710
www.counterpointpress.com

Printed in the United States of America

10 9 8 7 6 5

Contents

THINK
LITTLE

First there was Civil Rights, and then there was the War, and now it is the Environment. The first two of this sequence of causes have already risen to the top of the nation's consciousness and declined somewhat in a remarkably short time. I mention this in order to begin with what I believe to be a justifiable skepticism. For it seems to me that the Civil Rights Movement and the Peace Movement, as popular causes in the electronic age, have partaken far too much of the nature of fads. Not for all, certainly, but for too many they have been the fashionable politics of the moment. As causes they have been undertaken too much in ignorance; they have been too much simplified; they have been powered too much by impatience and guilt of conscience and short-term enthusiasm, and too little by an authentic social vision and long-term conviction and deliberation. For most people those causes have remained almost entirely abstract; there has been too little personal involvement, and too much involvement in organizations that were insisting that *other* organizations should do what was right.

There is considerable danger that the Environmental Movement will have the same nature: that it will be a public cause, served by organizations that will self-righteously criticize and condemn other organizations, inflated for a while by a lot of public talk in the media, only to be replaced in its turn by another fashionable crisis. I hope that will not happen, and I believe that there are ways to keep it from happening, but I know that if this effort is carried on solely as a public cause, if millions of people cannot or will not undertake it as a *private* cause as well, then it is *sure* to happen. In five years the energy of our present concern will have petered out in a series of public gestures – and no doubt in a series of empty laws – and a great, and perhaps the last, human opportunity will have been lost.

It need not be that way. A better possibility is that the movement to preserve the environment will be seen to be, as I think it has to be, not a digression from the civil rights and peace movements, but the logical culmination of those movements. For I believe that the separation of these three problems is artificial. They have the same cause, and that is the mentality of greed and exploitation. The mentality that exploits and destroys the natural environment is the same that abuses racial and economic minorities, that imposes on young men the tyranny of the military draft, that makes war against peasants and women and children with the indifference of technology. The mentality that destroys a watershed and then panics at the threat of flood is the same mentality that gives institutionalized insult to black people and then panics at the prospect of race riots. It is the same mentality that can mount deliberate warfare against a civilian population and then express moral shock at the logical consequence of such warfare at My Lai. We would be fools to believe that we could solve any one of these problems without solving the others.

To me, one of the most important aspects of the Environmental Movement is that it brings us not just to another public

crisis, but to a crisis of the protest movement itself. For the environmental crisis
should make it dramatically clear, as perhaps it has not always been before, that
there is no public crisis that is not also private. To most advocates of civil rights, racism has seemed mostly the fault of someone
else. For most advocates of peace, the war
has been a remote reality, and the burden of
the blame has seemed to rest mostly on the
government. I am certain that these crises
have been more private, and that we have
each suffered more from them and been
more responsible for them, than has been
readily apparent, but the connections have
been difficult to see. Racism and militar-
ism have been institutionalized among us
for too long for our personal involvement
in those evils to be easily apparent to us.
Think, for example, of all the Northerners
who assumed – until black people attempted

to move into *their* neighborhoods – that racism was a Southern phenomenon. And think how quickly – one might almost say how naturally – among some of its members the Peace Movement has spawned policies of deliberate provocation and violence.

BUT THE ENVIRONMENTAL crisis rises closer to home. Every time we draw a breath, every time we drink a glass of water, we are suffering from it. And more important, every time we indulge in, or depend on, the wastefulness of our economy – and our economy's first principle is waste – we are *causing* the crisis. Nearly every one of us, nearly every day of his life, is contributing *directly* to the ruin of this planet. A protest meeting on the issue of environmental abuse is not a convocation of accusers, it is a convocation of the guilty. That realization ought to clear the smog of self-righteousness that has almost conventionally hovered over these occasions and let us see the work that is to be done.

In this crisis it is certain that every one of us has a public responsibility. We must not cease to bother the government and the other institutions to see that they never become comfortable with easy promises. For myself, I want to say that I hope never again to go to Frankfort to present a petition to the governor on an issue so vital as that of strip mining, only to be dealt with by some ignorant functionary – as several of us were not so long ago, the governor himself being 'too busy' to receive us. Next time I will go prepared to wait as long as necessary to see that the petitioners' complaints and their arguments are heard *fully* – and by the governor. And then I will hope to find ways to keep those complaints and arguments from being forgotten until something is done to relieve them. The time is past when it was enough merely to elect our officials. We will have to elect them and then go and *watch* them and keep our hands on them, the way the coal companies do. We have made a tradition in Kentucky of putting self-servers, and worse, in charge of our vital interests. I am sick of it. And I think that one way to change it is to make Frankfort a less comfortable place. I believe in American political principles, and I will not sit idly by and see those principles destroyed by sorry practice. I am ashamed that American government should have become the chief cause of disillusionment with American principles.

And so when the government in Frankfort again proves too stupid or too blind or too corrupt to see the plain truth and to act with simple decency, I intend to be there, and I trust that I won't be alone. I hope, moreover, to be there, not with a sign or a slogan or a button, but with the facts and the arguments. A crowd whose discontent has risen no higher than the level of slogans is *only* a crowd. But a crowd that understands the reasons for its discontent and knows the remedies is a vital community, and it will have to be reckoned with. I would rather go before the government with two men who have a competent understanding of an issue, and who therefore deserve a hearing, than with two thousand who are vaguely dissatisfied.

But even the most articulate public protest is not enough. We don't live in the government or in institutions or in our public utterances and acts, and the environmental crisis has its roots in our *lives*. By the same token, environmental health will also be rooted in our lives. That is, I take it, simply a fact, and in the light of it we can see how superficial and foolish we would be to think that we could correct what is wrong merely by tinkering with the institutional machinery. The changes that are required are fundamental changes in the way we are living.

WHAT WE ARE up against in this country, in any attempt to invoke private responsibility, is that we have nearly destroyed private life. Our people have given up their independence in return for the cheap seductions and the shoddy merchandise of so-called 'affluence.' We have delegated all our vital functions and responsibilities to salesmen and agents and bureaus and experts of all sorts. We cannot feed or clothe ourselves, or entertain ourselves, or communicate with each other, or be charitable or neighborly or loving, or even respect ourselves, without recourse to a merchant or a corporation or a public service organization or an agency of the government or a style-setter or an expert. Most of us cannot think of dissenting from the opinions or the actions of one organization without first forming a new organization. Individualism is going around these days in uniform, handing out the party line on individualism. Dissenters want to publish their personal opinions over a thousand signatures.

The Confucian *Great Digest* says that the 'chief way for the production of wealth' (and it is talking about real goods, not money) is 'that the producers be many and that the mere consumers be few . . .' But even in the much-publicized rebellion of the young against the materialism of the affluent society, the consumer mentality is too often still intact: the standards of behavior are still those of kind and quantity, the security sought is still the security of numbers, and the chief motive is still the consumer's anxiety that he is missing out on what is 'in.' In this state of total consumerism – which is to say a state of helpless dependence on things and services and ideas and motives that we have forgotten how to provide ourselves – all meaningful contact between ourselves and the earth is broken. We do not understand the earth in terms either of what it offers us or of what it requires of us, and I think it is the rule that people inevitably destroy what they do not understand. Most of us are not directly responsible for strip mining and extractive agriculture and other forms of environmental abuse. But we are guilty nevertheless, for we connive in them by our ignorance. We are ignorantly dependent on them. We do not know enough about them; we do not have a particular enough sense of their danger. Most of us, for example, not only do not know how to produce the best food in the best way – we don't know how to produce any kind in any way. Our model citizen is a sophisticate who before puberty understands how to produce a baby, but who at the age of thirty will not know how to produce a potato. And for this condition we have elaborate rationalizations, instructing us that dependence for everything on somebody else is efficient and economical and a scientific miracle. I say, instead, that it is madness, mass produced. A man who understands the weather only in terms of golf is participating in a public insanity that either he or his descendants will be bound to realize as suffering. I believe that the death of the world is breeding in such minds much more certainly and much faster than in any political capital or atomic arsenal.

For an index of our loss of contact with the earth we need only look at the condition of the American farmer – who must enact our society's dependence on the land. In an age of unparalleled affluence and leisure, the American farmer is harder pressed and harder worked than ever before; his margin of profit is small, his hours are long; his outlays for land and equipment and the expenses of maintenance and operation are growing rapidly greater; he cannot compete with industry for labor; he is being forced more and more to depend on the use of destructive chemicals and on the wasteful methods of haste. As a class, farmers are one of the despised minorities. So far as I can see, farming is considered marginal or incidental to the economy of the country, and farmers, when they are thought of at all, are thought of as hicks and yokels, whose lives do not fit into the modern scene. The average American farmer is now an old man whose children have moved away to the cities. His knowledge, and his intimate connection with the land, are about to be lost. The small independent farmer is going the way of the small independent craftsmen and storekeepers. He is being forced off the land into the cities, his place taken by absentee owners, corporations, and machines. Some would justify all this in the name of efficiency. As I see it, it is an enormous social and economic and cultural blunder. For the small farmers who lived on their farms *cared* about their land. And given their established connection to their land – which was often hereditary and traditional as well as economic – they could have been encouraged to care for it more competently than they have so far. The corporations and machines that replace them will never be bound to the land by the sense of birthright and continuity, or by the love that enforces care. They will be bound by the rule of efficiency, which takes thought only of the volume of the year's produce, and takes no thought of the life of the land, not measurable in pounds or dollars, which will assure the livelihood and the health of the coming generations.

If we are to hope to correct our abuses of each other and of other races and of our land, and if our effort to correct these abuses is to be more than a political fad that will in the long run be only another form of abuse, then we are going to have to go far beyond public protest and political action. We are going to have to rebuild the substance and the integrity of private life in this country. We are going to have to gather up the fragments of knowledge and responsibility that we have parceled out to the bureaus and the corporations and the specialists, and put those fragments back together in our own minds and in our families and households and neighborhoods. We need better government, no doubt about it. But we also need better minds, better friendships, better marriages, better communities. We need persons and households that do not have to wait upon organizations, but can make necessary changes in themselves, on their own.

FOR MOST OF the history of this country our motto, implied or spoken, has been Think Big. A better motto, and an essential one now, is Think Little. That implies the necessary change of thinking and feeling, and suggests the necessary work. Thinking Big has led us to the two biggest and cheapest political dodges of our time: plan-making and law-making. The lotus-eaters of this era are in Washington, D.C., Thinking Big. Somebody perceives a problem, and somebody in the government comes up with a plan or a law. The result, mostly, has been the persistence of the problem, and the enlargement and enrichment of the government.

But the discipline of thought is not generalization; it is detail, and it is personal behavior. While the government is 'studying' and funding and organizing its Big Thought, nothing is being done. But the citizen who is willing to Think Little, and, accepting the discipline of that, to go ahead on his own, is already solving the problem. A man who is trying to live as a neighbor to his neighbors will have a lively and practical understanding of the work of peace and brotherhood, and let there be no mistake about it – he is *doing* that work. A couple who make a good marriage, and raise healthy, morally competent children, are serving the world's future more directly and surely than any political leader, though they never utter a public word. A good farmer who is dealing with the problem of soil erosion on an acre of ground has a sounder grasp of that problem and *cares* more about it and is probably doing more to solve it than any bureaucrat who is talking about it in general. A man who is willing to undertake the discipline and the difficulty of mending his own ways is worth more to the conservation movement than a hundred who are insisting merely that the government and the industries mend *their* ways.

IF YOU ARE concerned about the proliferation of trash, then by all means start an organization in your community to do something about it. But before – *and while* – you organize, pick up some cans and bottles yourself. That way, at least, you will assure yourself and others that you mean what you say. If you are concerned about air pollution, help push for government controls, but drive your car less, use less fuel in your home. If you are worried about the damming of wilderness rivers, join the

Sierra Club, write to the government, but turn off the lights you're not using, don't install an air conditioner, don't be a sucker for electrical gadgets, don't waste water. In other words, if you are fearful of the destruction of the environment, then learn to quit being an environmental parasite. We all are, in one way or another, and the remedies are not always obvious, though they certainly will always be difficult. They require a new kind of life – harder, more laborious, poorer in luxuries and gadgets, but also, I am certain, richer in meaning and more abundant in real pleasure. To have a healthy environment we will all have to give up things we like; we may even have to give up things we have come to think of as necessities. But to be fearful of the disease and yet unwilling to pay for the cure is not just to be hypocritical; it is to be doomed. If you talk a good line without being changed by what you say, then you are not just hyp-ocritical and doomed; you have become an agent of the disease. Consider, for an ex-ample, President Nixon, who advertises his grave concern about the destruction of the environment, and who turns up the air con-ditioner to make it cool enough to build a fire.

Odd as I am sure it will appear to some, I can think of no better form of personal involvement in the cure of the environment than that of gardening. A person who is growing a garden, if he is growing it organ-ically, is improving a piece of the world. He is producing something to eat, which makes him somewhat independent of the grocery business, but he is also enlarging, for him-self, the meaning of food and the pleasure of eating. The food he grows will be fresher, more nutritious, less contaminated by poi-sons and preservatives and dyes than what he can buy at a store. He is reducing the trash problem; a garden is not a disposable container, and it will digest and reuse its own wastes. If he enjoys working in his garden, then he is less dependent on an automobile or a merchant for his pleasure. He is involving himself directly in the work of feeding people.

If you think I'm wandering off the subject, let me remind you that most of the vegetables necessary for a family of four can be grown on a plot of forty by sixty feet. I think we might see in this an economic potential of considerable importance, since we now appear to be facing the possibility of widespread famine. How much food could be grown in the dooryards of cities and suburbs? How much could be grown along the extravagant right-of-ways of the interstate system? Or how much could be grown, by the intensive practices and economics of the

garden or small farm, on so-called marginal lands? Louis Bromfield liked to point
out that the people of France survived crisis after crisis because they were a nation
of gardeners, who in times of want turned
with great skill to their own small plots of
ground. And F. H. King, an agriculture pro-
fessor who traveled extensively in the Orient in 1907, talked to a Chinese farmer who
supported a family of twelve, 'one donkey,
one cow . . . and two pigs on 2.5 acres of
cultivated land' – and who did this, moreover, by agricultural methods that were
sound enough to have maintained his land
in prime fertility through several thousand
years of such use. These are possibilities
that are readily apparent and attractive to
minds that are prepared to Think Little. To
Big Thinkers – the bureaucrats and busi-
nessmen of agriculture – they are invisible.
But intensive, organic agriculture kept the

farms of the Orient thriving for thousands of years, whereas extensive – which is to say, exploitive or extractive – agriculture has critically reduced the fertility of American farmlands in a few centuries or even a few decades.

A person who undertakes to grow a garden at home, by practices that will preserve rather than exploit the economy of the soil, has set his mind decisively against what is wrong with us. He is helping himself in a way that dignifies him and that is rich in meaning and pleasure. But he is doing something else that is more important: he is making vital contact with the soil and the weather on which his life depends. He will no longer look upon rain as a traffic impediment, or upon the sun as a holiday decoration. And his sense of humanity's dependence on the world will have grown precise enough, one would hope, to be politically clarifying and useful.

WHAT I AM saying is that if we apply our minds directly and competently to the needs of the earth, then we will have begun to make fundamental and necessary changes in our minds. We will begin to understand and to mistrust *and to change* our wasteful economy, which markets not just the produce of the earth, but also the earth's ability to produce. We will see that beauty and utility are alike dependent upon the health of the world. But we will also see through the fads and the fashions of protest. We will see that war and oppression and pollution are not separate issues, but are aspects of the same issue. Amid the outcries for the liberation of this group or that, we will know that no person is free except in the freedom of other persons, and that our only real freedom is to know and faithfully occupy our place – a much humbler place than we have been taught to think – in the order of creation.

But the change of mind I am talking about involves not just a change of knowledge, but also a change of attitude toward our essential ignorance, a change in our bearing in the face of mystery. The principles of ecology, if we will take them to heart, should keep us aware that our lives depend upon other lives and upon processes and energies in an interlocking system that, though we can destroy it, we can neither fully understand nor fully control. And our great dangerousness is that, locked in our selfish and myopic economy, we have been willing to change or destroy far beyond our power to understand. We are not humble enough or reverent enough.

Some time ago, I heard a representative

of a paper company refer to conservation as a 'no-return investment.' This man's thinking was exclusively oriented to the annual profit of his industry. Circumscribed by the demand that the profit be great, he simply could not be answerable to any other demand – not even to the obvious needs of his own children.

Consider, in contrast, the profound ecological intelligence of Black Elk, 'a holy man of the Oglala Sioux,' who in telling his story said that it was not his own life that was important to him, but what he had shared with all life: 'It is the story of all life that is holy and it is good to tell, and of us two-leggeds sharing in it with the four-leggeds and the wings of the air and all green things . . .' And of the great vision that came to him when he was a child he said: 'I saw that the sacred hoop of my people was one of many hoops that made one circle, wide as daylight and as starlight, and in the center grew one mighty flowering tree to shelter all the children of one mother and father. And I saw that it was holy.'

(1970)

A NATIVE HILL

Pull down thy vanity, it is not man
Made courage, or made order, or
        made grace,
Pull down thy vanity, I say pull down.
Learn of the green-world what can
        be thy place . . .
        EZRA POUND, *Canto LXXXI*

1

THE HILL IS not a hill in the usual sense. It
has no 'other side.' It is an arm of Kentucky's
central upland known as The Bluegrass; one

can think of it as a ridge reaching out from that center, progressively cut and divided, made ever narrower by the valleys of the creeks that drain it. The town of Port Royal in Henry County stands on one of the last heights of this upland, the valleys of two creeks, Gullion's Branch and Cane Run, opening on either side of it into the valley of the Kentucky River. My house backs against the hill's foot where it descends from the town to the river. The river, whose waters have carved the hill and so descended from it, lies within a hundred steps of my door.

Within about four miles of Port Royal, on the upland and in the bottoms upriver, all my grandparents and great-grandparents lived and left such memories as their descendants have bothered to keep. Little enough has been remembered. The family's life here goes back to my mother's great-great-grandfather and to my father's great-grandfather, but of those earliest ones there are only a few vague word-of-mouth recollections. The only place antecedent to this place that has any immediacy to any of us is the town of Cashel in County Tipperary, Ireland, which one of my great-grandfathers left as a boy to spend the rest of his life in Port Royal. His name was James Mathews, and he was a shoemaker. So well did he fit his life into this place that he is remembered, even in the family, as having belonged here. The family's only real memories of Cashel are my own, coming from a short visit I made there five years ago.

And so, such history as my family has is the history of its life here. All that any of us may know of ourselves is to be known in relation to this place. And since I did most of my growing up here, and have had most of my most meaningful experiences here, the place and the history, for me, have been inseparable, and there is a sense in which my own life is inseparable from the history and the place. It is a complex inheritance, and I have been both enriched and bewildered by it.

I BEGAN MY life as the old times and the last of the old-time people were dying out. The Depression and World War II delayed the mechanization of the farms here, and one of the first disciplines imposed on me was that of a teamster. Perhaps I first stood in the role of student before my father's father, who, halting a team in front of me, would demand to know which mule had the best head, which the best shoulder or rump, which was the lead mule, were they hitched right. And there came a time when I knew, and took a considerable pride in knowing. Having a boy's usual desire to play at what he sees men working at, I learned to harness and hitch and work a team. I felt distinguished by that, and took the same pride in it that other boys my age took in their knowledge of automobiles. I seem to have been born with an aptitude for a way of life that was doomed, although I did not understand that at the time. Free of any intuition of its doom, I delighted in it, and learned all I could about it.

That knowledge, and the men who gave it to me, influenced me deeply. It entered my imagination, and gave its substance and tone to my mind. It fashioned in me possibilities and limits, desires and frustrations, that I do not expect to live to the end of. And it is strange to think how barely in the nick of time it came to me. If I had been born five years later I would have begun in a different world, and would no doubt have become a different man.

Those five years made a critical difference in my life, and it is a historical difference. One of the results is that in my generation I am something of an anachronism. I am less a child of my time than the people of my age who grew up in the cities, or than the people who grew up here in my own place five years after I did. In my acceptance of twentieth-century realities there has had to be a certain deliberateness, whereas most of my contemporaries had them simply by being born to them.

IN MY TEENS, when I was away at school, I could comfort myself by recalling in intricate detail the fields I had worked and played in, and hunted over, and ridden through on horseback – and that were richly associated in my mind with people and with stories. I could recall even the casual locations of certain small rocks. I could recall the look of a hundred different kinds of daylight on all those places, the look of animals grazing over them, the postures and attitudes and movements of the men who worked in them, the quality of the grass and the crops that had grown on them. I had come to be aware of it as one is aware of one's body; it was present to me whether I thought of it or not.

When I have thought of the welfare of the earth, the problems of its health and preservation, the care of its life, I have had this place before me, the part representing the whole more vividly and accurately, making clearer and more pressing demands, than any *idea* of the whole. When I have thought of kindness or cruelty, weariness or exuberance, devotion or betrayal, carelessness or care, doggedness or awkwardness or grace, I have had in my mind's eye the men and women of this place, their faces and gestures and movements.

I HAVE PONDERED a great deal over a conversation I took part in a number of years ago in one of the offices of New York University. I had lived away from Kentucky for several years – in California, in Europe, in New York City. And now I had decided to go back and take a teaching job at the University of Kentucky, giving up the position I then held on the New York University faculty. That day I had been summoned by one of my superiors at the university, whose intention, I had already learned, was to persuade me to stay on in New York 'for my own good.'

The decision to leave had cost me considerable difficulty and doubt and hard thought – for hadn't I achieved what had become one of the almost traditional goals of American writers? I had reached the greatest city in the nation; I had a good job; I was meeting other writers and talking with them and learning from them; I had reason to hope that I might take a still larger part in the literary life of that place. On the other hand, I knew I had not escaped Kentucky, and had never really wanted to. I was still writing about it, and had recognized that I would probably need to write about it for the rest of my life. Kentucky was my fate – not an altogether pleasant fate, though it had much that was pleasing in it, but one that I could not leave behind simply by going to another place, and that I therefore felt more and more obligated to meet directly and to understand. Perhaps even more important, I still had a deep love for the place I had been born in, and liked the idea of going back to be part of it again. And that, too, I felt obligated to try to understand. Why should I love one place so much more than any other? What could be the meaning or use of such love?

The elder of the faculty began the conversation by alluding to Thomas Wolfe, who once taught at the same institution. 'Young man,' he said, 'don't you know you can't go home again?' And he went on to speak of the advantages, for a young writer, of living in New York among the writers and the editors and the publishers.

The conversation that followed was a persistence of politeness in the face of impossibility. I knew as well as Wolfe that there is a certain *metaphorical* sense in which you can't go home again – that is, the past is lost to the extent that it cannot be lived in again. I knew perfectly well that I could not return home and be a child, or recover the secure pleasures of childhood. But I knew also that as the sentence was spoken to me it bore a self-dramatizing sentimentality that was absurd. Home – the place, the countryside – was still there, still pretty much as I left it, and there was no reason I could not go back to it if I wanted to.

As for the literary world, I had ventured some distance into that, and liked it well enough. I knew that because I was a writer the literary world would always have an importance for me and would always attract my interest. But I never doubted that the world was more important to me than the literary world; and the world would always be most fully and clearly present to me in the place I was fated by birth to know better than any other.

And so I had already chosen according to the most intimate and necessary inclinations of my own life. But what keeps me thinking of that conversation is the feeling that it was a confrontation of two radically different minds, and that it was a confrontation with significant historical overtones.

I do not pretend to know all about the other man's mind, but it was clear that he wished to speak to me as a representative of the literary world – the world he assumed that I aspired to above all others. His argument was based on the belief that once one had attained the metropolis, the literary capital, the worth of one's origins was canceled out; there simply could be nothing *worth* going back to. What lay behind one had ceased to be a part of life, and had become 'subject matter.' And there was the belief, long honored among American intellectuals and artists and writers, that a place such as I came from could be returned to only at the price of intellectual death; cut off from the cultural springs of the metropolis, the American countryside is Circe and Mammon. Finally, there was the assumption that the life of the metropolis is *the* experience, the *modern* experience, and that the life of the rural towns, the farms, the wilderness places is not only irrelevant to our time, but archaic as well because unknown or unconsidered by the people who really matter – that is, the urban intellectuals.

I was to realize during the next few years how false and destructive and silly those ideas are. But even then I was aware that life outside the literary world was not without honorable precedent: if there was Wolfe, there was also Faulkner; if there was James, there was also Thoreau. But what I had in my mind that made the greatest difference was the knowledge of the few square miles in Kentucky that were mine by inheritance and by birth and by the intimacy the mind makes with the place it awakens in.

WHAT FINALLY FREED me from these doubts and suspicions was the insistence in what was happening to me that, far from being bored and diminished and obscured to myself by my life here, I had grown more alive and more conscious than I had ever been.

I had made a significant change in my relation to the place: before, it had been mine by coincidence or accident; now it was mine by choice. My return, which at first had been hesitant and tentative, grew wholehearted and sure. I had come back to stay. I hoped to live here the rest of my life. And once that was settled I began to *see* the place with a new clarity and a new understanding and a new seriousness. Before coming back I had been willing to allow the possibility – which one of my friends insisted on – that I already knew this place as well as I ever would. But now I began to see the real abundance and richness of it. It is, I saw, inexhaustible in its history, in the details of its life, in its possibilities. I walked over it, looking, listening, smelling, touching, alive to it as never before. I listened to the talk of my kinsmen and neighbors as I never had done, alert to their knowledge of the place, and to the qualities and energies of their speech. I began more seriously than ever to learn the names of things – the wild plants and animals, the natural processes, the local places – and to articulate my observations and memories. My language increased and strengthened, and sent my mind into the place like a live root system. And so what has become the usual order of things reversed itself with me; my mind became the root of my life rather than its sublimation. I came to see myself as growing out of the earth like the other native animals and plants. I saw my body and my daily motions as brief coherences and articulations of the energy of the place, which would fall back into it like leaves in the autumn.

IN THIS AWAKENING there has been a good deal of pain. When I lived in other places I looked on their evils with the curious eye of a traveler; I was not responsible for them; it cost me nothing to be a critic, for I had not been there long, and I did not feel that I would stay. But here, now that I am both native and citizen, there is no immunity to what is wrong. It is impossible to escape the sense that I am involved in history. What I am has been to a considerable extent determined by what my forebears were, by how they chose to treat this place while they lived in it; the lives of most of them diminished it, and limited its possibilities, and narrowed its future. And every day I am confronted by the question of what inheritance I will leave. What do I have that I am using up? For it has been our history that each generation in this place has been less welcome to it than the last. There has been less here for them. At each arrival there has been less fertility in the soil, and a larger inheritance of destructive precedent and shameful history.

I am forever being crept up on and newly startled by the realization that my people established themselves here by killing or driving out the original possessors, by the awareness that people were once bought and sold here by my people, by the sense of the violence they have done to their own kind and to each other and to the earth, by the evidence of their persistent failure to serve either the place or their own community in it. I am forced, against all my hopes and inclinations, to regard the history of my people here as the progress of the doom of what I value most in the world: the life and health of the earth, the peacefulness of human communities and households.

And so here, in the place I love more than any other and where I have chosen among all other places to live my life, I am more painfully divided within myself than I could be in any other place.

I know of no better key to what is adverse in our heritage in this place than the account of 'The Battle of the Fire-Brands,' quoted in Collins's *History of Kentucky* 'from the autobiography of Rev. Jacob Young, a Methodist minister.' The 'Newcastle' referred to is the present-day New Castle, the county seat of Henry County. I give the quote in full:

The costume of the Kentuckians was a hunting shirt, buckskin pantaloons, a leathern belt around their middle, a scabbard, and a big knife fastened to their belt; some of them wore hats and some caps. Their feet were covered with moccasins, made of dressed deer skins. They did not think themselves dressed without their powder-horn and shot-pouch, or the gun and the tomahawk. They were ready, then, for all alarms. They knew but little. They could clear ground, raise corn, and kill turkeys, deer, bears, and buffalo; and, when it became necessary, they understood the art of fighting the Indians as well as any men in the United States.

Shortly after we had taken up our residence, I was called upon to assist in opening a road from the place where Newcastle now stands, to the mouth of Kentucky river. That country, then, was an unbroken forest; there was nothing but an Indian trail passing the wilderness. I met the company early in the morning, with my axe, three days' provisions, and my knapsack. Here I found a captain, with about 100 men, all prepared to labor; about as jovial a company as I ever saw, all good-natured and civil. This was about the last of November, 1797. The day was cold and clear. The country through which the company passed was delightful; it was not a flat country, but, what the Kentuckians called, rolling ground – was quite well stored with lofty timber, and the undergrowth was very pretty. The beautiful canebrakes gave it a peculiar charm. What rendered it most interesting was the great abundance of wild turkeys, deer, bears, and other wild animals. The company worked hard all day, in quiet, and every man obeyed the captain's orders punctually.

About sundown, the captain, after a short address, told us the night was going to be very cold, and we must make very large fires.

We felled the hickory trees in great abundance; made great log-heaps, mixing the dry wood with the green hickory; and, laying down a kind of sleepers under the pile, elevated the heap and caused it to burn rapidly. Every man had a water vessel in his knapsack; we searched for and found a stream of water. By this time, the fires were showing to great advantage; so we warmed our cold victuals, ate our suppers, and spent the evening in hearing the hunter's stories relative to the bloody scenes of the Indian war. We then heard some pretty fine singing, considering the circumstances.

Thus far, well; but a change began to take place. They became very rude, and raised the war-whoop. Their shrill shrieks made me tremble.

They chose two captains, divided the men into two companies, and commenced fighting with the firebrands – the log heaps having burned down. The only law for their government was, that no man should throw a brand without fire on it – so that they might know how to dodge. They fought, for two or three hours, in perfect good nature; till brands became scarce, and they began to violate the law. Some were severely wounded, blood began to flow freely, and they were in a fair way of commencing a fight in earnest. At this moment, the loud voice of the captain rang out above the din, ordering every man to retire to rest. They dropped their weapons of warfare, rekindled the fires, and laid down to sleep. We finished our road according to directions, and returned home in health and peace.

THE SIGNIFICANCE OF this bit of history is in its utter violence. The work of clearing the road was itself violent. And from the orderly violence of that labor, these men turned for amusement to disorderly violence. They were men whose element was violence; the only alternatives they were aware of were those within the comprehension of main strength. And let us acknowledge that these were the truly influential men in the history of Kentucky, as well as in the history of most of the rest of America. In comparison to the fatherhood of such as these, the so-called 'founding fathers' who established our political ideals are but distant cousins. It is not John Adams or Thomas Jefferson whom we see night after night in the magic mirror of the television set; we see these builders of the road from New Castle to the mouth of the Kentucky River. Their reckless violence has glamorized all our trivialities and evils. Their aggressions have simplified our complexities and problems. They have cut all our Gordian knots. They have appeared in all our disguises and costumes. They have worn all our uniforms. Their war whoop has sanctified our inhumanity and ratified our blunders of policy.

To testify to the persistence of their influence, it is only necessary for me to confess that I read the Reverend Young's account of them with delight; I yield a considerable admiration to the exuberance and extravagance of their fight with the firebrands; I take a certain pride in belonging to the same history and the same place that they belong to – though I know that they represent the worst that is in us, and in me, and that their presence in our history has been ruinous, and that their survival among us promises ruin.

'They knew but little,' the observant Reverend says of them, and this is the most suggestive thing he says. It is surely understandable and pardonable, under the circumstances, that these men were ignorant by the standards of formal schooling. But one immediately reflects that the American Indian, who was ignorant by the same standards, nevertheless knew how to live in the country without making violence the invariable mode of his relation to it; in fact, from the ecologist's or the conservationist's point of view, he did it *no* violence. This is because he had, in place of what we would call education, a fully integrated culture, the content of which was a highly complex sense of his dependence on the earth. The same, I believe, was generally true of the peasants of certain old agricultural societies, particularly in the Orient. They belonged by an intricate awareness to the earth they lived on and by, which meant that they respected it, which meant that they practiced strict economies in the use of it.

The abilities of those Kentucky road builders of 1797 were far more primitive and rudimentary than those of the Stone Age people they had driven out. They could clear the ground, grow corn, kill game, and make war. In the minds and hands of men who 'know but little' – or little else – all of these abilities are certain to be destructive, even of those values and benefits their use may be intended to serve.

On such a night as the Reverend Young describes, an Indian would have made do with a small shelter and a small fire. But these road builders, veterans of the Indian War, 'felled the hickory trees in great abundance; made great log-heaps . . . and caused

[them] to burn rapidly.' Far from making a small shelter that could be adequately heated by a small fire, their way was to make no shelter at all, and heat instead a sizable area of the landscape. The idea was that when faced with abundance one should consume abundantly – an idea that has survived to become the basis of our present economy. It is neither natural nor civilized, and even from a 'practical' point of view it is to the last degree brutalizing and stupid.

I think that the comparison of these road builders with the Indians, on the one hand, and with Old World peasants on the other, is a most suggestive one. The Indians and the peasants were people who belonged deeply and intricately to their places. Their ways of life had evolved slowly in accordance with their knowledge of their land, of its needs, of their own relation of dependence and responsibility to it. The road builders, on the contrary, were *placeless* people. That is why they 'knew but little.' Having left Europe far behind, they had not yet in any meaningful sense arrived in America, not yet having *devoted* themselves to any part of it in a way that would produce the intricate knowledge of it necessary to live in it without destroying it. Because they belonged to no place, it was almost inevitable that they should behave violently toward the places they came to. We *still* have not, in any meaningful way, arrived in America. And in spite of our great reservoir of facts and methods, in comparison to the deep earthly wisdom of established peoples we still know but little.

But my understanding of this curiously parabolic fragment of history will not be complete until I have considered more directly that the occasion of this particular violence was the building of a road. It is obvious that one who values the idea of community cannot speak against roads without risking all sorts of absurdity. It must be noticed, nevertheless, that the predecessor to this first road was 'nothing but an Indian trail passing the wilderness' – a path. The Indians, then, who had the wisdom and the grace to live in this country for perhaps ten thousand years without destroying or damaging any of it, needed for their travels no more than a footpath; but their successors, who in a century and a half plundered the area of at least half its topsoil and virtually all of its forest, felt immediately that they had to have a road. My interest is not in the question of whether or not they *needed* the road, but in the fact that the road was then, and is now, the most characteristic form of their relation to the country.

The difference between a path and a road is not only the obvious one. A path is little more than a habit that comes with knowledge of a place. It is a sort of ritual of familiarity. As a form, it is a form of contact with a known landscape. It is not destructive. It is the perfect adaptation, through experience and familiarity, of movement to place; it obeys the natural contours; such obstacles as it meets it goes around. A road, on the other hand, even the most primitive road, embodies a resistance against the landscape. Its reason is not simply the necessity for movement, but haste. Its wish is to *avoid* contact with the landscape; it seeks so far as possible to go over the country, rather than through it; its aspiration, as we see clearly in the example of our modern freeways, is to be a bridge; its tendency is to translate place into space in order to traverse it with the least effort. It is destructive, seeking to remove or destroy all obstacles in its way. The primitive road advanced by the destruction of the forest; modern roads advance by the destruction of topography.

That first road from the site of New Castle to the mouth of the Kentucky River – lost now either by obsolescence or metamorphosis – is now being crossed and to some extent replaced by its modern descendant known as 1–71, and I have no wish to disturb the question of whether or not *this* road was needed. I only want to observe that it bears no relation whatever to the country it passes through. It is a pure abstraction, built to serve the two abstractions that are the poles of our national life: commerce and expensive pleasure. It was built, not according to the lay of the land, but according to a blueprint. Such homes and farmlands and woodlands as happened to be in its way are now buried under it. A part of a hill near here

that would have caused it to turn aside
was simply cut down and disposed of as
thoughtlessly as the pioneer road builders
would have disposed of a tree. Its form
is the form of speed, dissatisfaction, and
anxiety. It represents the ultimate in en-
gineering sophistication, but the crudest
possible valuation of life in this world. It
is as adequate a symbol of our relation to
our country now as that first road was of
our relation to it in 1797.

BUT THE SENSE of the past also gives a
deep richness and resonance to nearly everything I see here. It is partly the sense
that what I now see, other men that I
have known once saw, and partly that this
knowledge provides an imaginative access
to what I do not know. I think of the country as a kind of palimpsest scrawled over
with the comings and goings of people, the

erasure of time already in process even as the marks of passage are put down. There are the ritual marks of neighborhood – roads, paths between houses. There are the domestic paths from house to barns and outbuildings and gardens, farm roads threading the pasture gates. There are the wanderings of hunters and searchers after lost stock, and the speculative or meditative or inquisitive 'walking around' of farmers on wet days and Sundays. There is the spiraling geometry of the rounds of implements in fields, and the passing and returning scratches of plows across croplands. Often these have filled an interval, an opening, between the retreat of the forest from the virgin ground and the forest's return to ground that has been worn out and given up. In the woods here one often finds cairns of stones picked up out of furrows, gullies left by bad farming, forgotten roads, stone chimneys of houses long rotted away or burned.

OCCASIONALLY ONE STUMBLES into a coincidence that, like an unexpected alignment of windows, momentarily cancels out the sense of historical whereabouts, giving with an overwhelming immediacy an awareness of the reality of the past.

The possibility of this awareness is always immanent in old homesites. It may suddenly bear in upon one at the sight of old orchard trees standing in the dooryard of a house now filled with baled hay. It came to me when I looked out the attic window of a disintegrating log house and saw a far view of the cleared ridges with wooded hollows in between, and nothing in sight to reveal the date. Who was I, leaning to the window? When?

It broke upon me one afternoon when,

walking in the woods on one of my family places, I came upon a gap in a fence, wired shut, but with deep-cut wagon tracks still passing through it under the weed growth and the fallen leaves. Where that thicket stands there was crop ground, maybe as late as my own time. I knew some of the men who tended it; their names and faces were instantly alive in my mind. I knew how it had been with them – how they would harness their mule teams in the early mornings in my grandfather's big barn and come to the woods-rimmed tobacco patches, the mules' feet wet with the dew. And in the solitude and silence that came upon them they would set to work, their water jugs left in the shade of bushes in the fencerows.

As a child I learned the early mornings in these places for myself, riding out in the wagons with the tobacco-cutting crews to those steep fields in the dew-wet shadow of the woods. As the day went on the shadow would draw back under the feet of the trees, and it would get hot. Little whirlwinds would cross the opening, picking up the dust and the dry 'ground leaves' of the tobacco. We made a game of running with my grandfather to stand, shoulders scrunched and eyes squinched, in their middles.

Having such memories, I can acknowledge only with reluctance and sorrow that those slopes should never have been broken. Rich as they were, they were too steep. The humus stood dark and heavy over them once; the plow was its doom.

EARLY ONE FEBRUARY morning in thick fog and spattering rain I stood on the riverbank and listened to a towboat working its way downstream. Its engines were idling, nudging cautiously through the fog into the Cane Run bend. The end of the head barge emerged finally like a shadow, and then the second barge appeared, and then the tow-boat itself. They made the bend, increased power, and went thumping off out of sight into the fog again.

Because the valley was so enclosed in fog, the boat with its tow appearing and disappearing again into the muffling whiteness within two hundred yards, the moment had a curious ambiguity. It was as though I was not necessarily myself at all. I could have been my grandfather, in his time, standing there watching, as I knew he had.

2

I START DOWN from one of the heights of the upland, the town of Port Royal at my back. It is a winter day, overcast and still, and the town is closed in itself, humming and muttering a little, like a winter beehive.

The dog runs ahead, prancing and

looking back, knowing the way we are about to go. This is a walk well established with us – a route in our minds as well as on the ground. There is a sort of mystery in the establishment of these ways. Anytime one crosses a given stretch of country with some frequency, no matter how wanderingly one begins, the tendency is always toward habit. By the third or fourth trip, without realizing it, one is following a fixed path, going the way one went before. After that, one may still wander, but only by deliberation, and when there is reason to hurry, or when the mind wanders rather than the feet, one returns to the old route. Familiarity has begun. One has made a relationship with the landscape, and the form and the symbol and the enactment of the relationship is the path. These paths of mine are seldom worn on the ground. They are habits of mind, directions and turns.

They are as personal as old shoes. My feet are comfortable in them.

From the height I can see far out over the country, the long open ridges of the farm-land, the wooded notches of the streams, the valley of the river opening beyond, and then more ridges and hollows of the same kind.

Underlying this country, nine hundred feet below the highest ridgetops, more than four hundred feet below the surface of the river, is sea level. We seldom think of it here; we are a long way from the coast, and the sea is alien to us. And yet the attraction of sea level dwells in this country as an ideal dwells in a man's mind. All our rains go in search of it and, departing, they have carved the land in a shape that is fluent and falling. The streams branch like vines, and between the branches the land rises steeply and then rounds and gentles into the long narrowing fingers of ridgeland. Near the heads of the streams even the steepest land was not too long ago farmed and kept cleared. But now it has been given up and the woods is returning. The wild is flowing back like a tide. The arable ridgetops reach out above the gathered trees like headlands into the sea, bearing their human burdens of fences and houses and barns, crops and roads.

Looking out over the country, one gets a sense of the whole of it: the ridges and hollows, the clustered buildings of the farms, the open fields, the woods, the stock ponds set like coins into the slopes. But this is a surface sense, an exterior sense, such as you get from looking down on the roof of a house. The height is a threshold from which to step down into the wooded folds of the land, the interior, under the trees and along the branching streams.

I pass through a pasture gate on a

deep-worn path that grows shallow a little way beyond, and then disappears altogether into the grass. The gate has gathered thousands of passings to and fro that have divided like the slats of a fan on either side of it. It is like a fist holding together the strands of a net.

Beyond the gate the land leans always more steeply toward the branch. I follow it down, and then bear left along the crease at the bottom of the slope. I have entered the downflow of the land. The way I am going is the way the water goes. There is something comfortable and fit-feeling in this, something free in this yielding to gravity and taking the shortest way down.

As the hollow deepens into the hill, before it has yet entered the woods, the grassy crease becomes a raw gully, and along the steepening slopes on either side I can see the old scars of erosion, places where the earth is gone clear to the rock. My people's errors have become the features of my country.

It occurs to me that it is no longer possible to imagine how this country looked in the beginning, before the white people drove their plows into it. It is not possible to know what was the shape of the land here in this hollow when it was first cleared. Too much of it is gone, loosened by the plows and washed away by the rain. I am walking the route of the departure of the virgin soil of the hill. I am not looking at the same land the firstcomers saw. The original surface of the hill is as extinct as the passenger pigeon. The pristine America that the first white man saw is a lost continent, sunk like Atlantis in the sea. The thought of what was here once and is gone forever will not leave me as long as I live. It is as though I walk knee-deep in its absence.

The slopes along the hollow steepen

still more, and I go in under the trees. I pass beneath the surface. I am enclosed, and my sense, my interior sense, of the country becomes intricate. There is no longer the possibility of seeing very far. The distances are closed off by the trees and the steepening walls of the hollow. One cannot grow familiar here by sitting and looking as one can up in the open on the ridge. Here the eyes become dependent on the feet. To see the woods from the inside one must look and move and look again. It is inexhaustible in its standpoints. A lifetime will not be enough to experience it all. Not far from the beginning of the woods, and set deep in the earth in the bottom of the hollow, is a rock-walled pool not a lot bigger than a bathtub. The wall is still nearly as straight and tight as when it was built. It makes a neatly turned narrow horseshoe, the open end downstream. This is a historical ruin, dug here either to catch and hold the water of the little branch, or to collect the water of a spring whose vein broke to the surface here – it is probably no longer possible to know which. The pool is filled with earth now, and grass grows in it. And the branch bends around it, cut down to the bare rock, a torrent after heavy rain, other times bone dry. All that is certain is that when the pool was dug and walled there was deep topsoil on the hill to gather and hold the water. And this high up, at least, the bottom of the hollow, instead of the present raw notch of the streambed, wore the same mantle of soil as the slopes, and the stream was a steady seep or trickle, running most or all of the year. This tiny pool no doubt once furnished water for a considerable number of stock through the hot summers. And now it is only a lost souvenir, archaic and useless, except for the bitter intelligence there is in it. It is one of the monuments to what is lost.

Wherever one goes along the streams of this part of the country, one is apt to come upon this old stonework. There are walled springs and pools. There are the walls built in the steeper hollows where the fences cross or used to cross; the streams have drifted dirt in behind them, so that now where they are still intact they make waterfalls that have scooped out small pools at their feet. And there used to be miles of stone fences, now mostly scattered and sifted back into the ground.

Considering these, one senses a historical patience, now also extinct in the country. These walls were built by men working long days for little wages, or by slaves. It was work that could not be hurried at, a meticulous finding and fitting together, as though reconstructing a previous wall that had been broken up and scattered like puzzle pieces. The wall would advance only a few yards a day. The pace of it could not be borne by most modern men, even if the wages could be afforded. Those men had to move in closer accord with their own rhythms, and nature's, than we do. They had no machines. Their capacities were only those of flesh and blood. They talked as they worked. They joked and laughed. They sang. The work was exacting and heavy and hard and slow. No opportunity for pleasure was missed or slighted. The days and the years were long. The work was long. At the end of this job the next would begin. Therefore, be patient. Such pleasure as there is, is here, now. Take pleasure as it comes. Take work as it comes. The end may never come, or when it does it may be the wrong end.

Now the men who built the walls and the men who had them built have long gone underground to be, along with the buried ledges and the roots and the burrowing animals, a part of the nature of the place in the minds of the ones who come after them. I think of them lying still in their graves, as level as the sills and thresholds of their lives, as though resisting to the last the slant of the ground. And their old walls, too, reenter nature, collecting lichens and mosses with patience their builders never conceived.

Like the pasture gates, the streams are great collectors of comings and goings. The streams go down, and paths always go down beside the streams. For a while I walk along an old wagon road that is buried in leaves – a fragment, beginningless and endless as the middle of a sentence on some scrap of papyrus. There is a cedar whose branches reach over this road, and under the branches I find the leavings of two kills of some bird of prey. The most recent is a pile of blue jay feathers. The other has been rained on and is not identifiable. How little we know. How little of this was intended or expected by any man. The road that has become the grave of men's passages has led to the life of the woods.

And I say to myself: Here is your road
without beginning or end, appearing
out of the earth and ending in it,
    bearing
no load but the hawk's kill, and the
    leaves
building earth on it, something more
to be borne. Tracks fill with earth
and return to absence. The road was
    worn
by men bearing earth along it. They
    have come
to endlessness. In their passing
they could not stay in, trees have risen

and stand still. It is leading to the
    dark,
to mornings where you are not. Here
is your road, beginningless and end-
    less as God.

NOW I HAVE come down within the sound
of the water. The winter has been rainy, and
the hill is full of dark seeps and trickles,
gathering finally, along these creases, into
flowing streams. The sound of them is one
of the elements, and defines a zone. When
their voices return to the hill after their absence during summer and autumn, it is a
better place to be. A thirst in the mind is
quenched.

I have already passed the place where
water began to flow in the little streambed I
am following. It broke into the light from beneath a rock ledge, a thin glittering stream.
It lies beside me as I walk, overtaking me

and going by, yet not moving, a thread of light and sound. And now from below comes the steady tumble and rush of the water of Camp Branch – whose nameless camp was it named for? – and gradually as I descend the sound of the smaller stream is lost in the sound of the larger.

The two hollows join, the line of the meeting of the two spaces obscured even in winter by the trees. But the two streams meet precisely as two roads. That is, the stream*beds* do; the one ends in the other. As for the meeting of the waters, there is no looking at that. The one flow does not end in the other, but continues in it, one with it, two clarities merged without a shadow.

All waters are one. This is a reach of the sea, flung like a net over the hill, and now drawn back to the sea. And as the sea is never raised in the earthly nets of fishermen, so the hill is never caught and pulled down by the watery net of the sea. But always a little of it is. Each of the gathering strands of the net carries back some of the hill melted in it. Sometimes, as now, it carries so little that the water flows clear; sometimes it carries a lot and is brown and heavy with it. Whenever greedy or thoughtless men have lived on it, the hill has literally flowed out of their tracks into the bottom of the sea.

There appears to be a law that when creatures have reached the level of consciousness, as men have, they must become conscious of the creation; they must learn how they fit into it and what its needs are and what it requires of them, or else pay a terrible penalty: the spirit of the creation will go out of them, and they will become destructive; the very earth will depart from them and go where they cannot follow.

My mind is never empty or idle at the joinings of streams. Here is the work of the world going on. The creation is felt, alive and intent on its materials, in such places. In the angle of the meeting of the two streams stands the steep wooded point of the ridge, like the prow of an up-turned boat – finished, as it was a thousand years ago, as it will be in a thousand years. Its becoming is only incidental to its being. It will be because it is. It has no aim or end except to be. By being, it is growing and wearing into what it will be. The fork of the stream lies at the foot of the slope like hammer and chisel laid down at the foot of a finished sculpture. But the stream is no dead tool; it is alive, it is still at its work. Put your hand to it to learn the health of this part of the world. It is the wrist of the hill.

Perhaps it is to prepare to hear someday the music of the spheres that I am always turning my ears to the music of streams. There is indeed a music in streams, but it is not for the hurried. It has to be loitered by and imagined. Or imagined *toward*, for it is hardly for men at all. Nature has a patient ear. To her the slowest funeral march sounds like a jig. She is satisfied to have the notes drawn out to the lengths of days or weeks or months. Small variations are acceptable to her, modulations as leisurely as the opening of a flower.

The stream is full of stops and gates. Here it has piled up rocks in its path, and pours over them into a tiny pool it has scooped at the foot of its fall. Here it has been dammed by a mat of leaves caught behind a fallen limb. Here it must force a narrow passage, here a wider one. Tomorrow the flow may increase or slacken, and the tone will shift. In an hour or a week that rock may give way, and the composition will advance by another note. Some idea of it may be got by walking slowly along and noting the changes as one passes from one little fall or rapid to another. But this is a highly simplified and diluted version of the real thing, which is too complex and widespread ever to be actually heard by us. The ear must imagine an impossible patience in order to grasp even the unimaginableness of such music.

But the creation is musical, and this is a part of its music, as birdsong is, or the words of poets. The music of the streams is the music of the shaping of the earth, by which the rocks are pushed and shifted downward toward the level of the sea.

And now I find an empty beer can lying in the path. This is the track of the ubiquitous man Friday of all our woods. In my walks I never fail to discover some sign that he has preceded me. I find his empty shotgun shells, his empty cans and bottles, his sandwich wrappings. In wooded places along roadsides one is apt to find, as well, his overtraveled bedsprings, his outcast refrigerator, and heaps of the imperishable refuse of his modern kitchen. A year ago, almost in this same place where I have found his beer can, I found a possum that he had shot dead and left lying, in celebration of his manhood. He is the true American pioneer, perfectly at rest in his assumption that he is the first and the last whose inheritance and fate this place will ever be. Going forth, as he may think, to sow, he only broadcasts his effects.

As I go on down the path alongside Camp Branch, I walk by the edge of croplands abandoned only within my own lifetime. On my left are the south slopes where the woods is old, long undisturbed. On my right, the more fertile north slopes are covered with patches of briars and sumacs and a lot of young walnut trees. Tobacco of an extraordinary quality was once grown here, and then the soil wore thin, and these places were given up for the more accessible ridges that were not so steep, where row cropping made better sense anyway. But now, under the thicket growth, a mat of bluegrass has grown to testify to the good nature of this ground. It was fine dirt that lay here once, and I am far from being able to say that I could have resisted the temptation to plow it. My understanding of what is best for it is the tragic understanding of hindsight, the awareness that I have been taught what was here to be lost by the loss of it.

We have lived by the assumption that what was good for us would be good for the world. And this has been based on the even flimsier assumption that we could know with any certainty what was good even for us. We have fulfilled the danger of this by making our personal pride and greed the standard of our behavior toward the world – to the incalculable disadvantage of the world and every living thing in it. And now, perhaps very close to too late, our great error has become clear. It is not only our own creativity – our own capacity for life – that is stifled by our arrogant assumption; the creation itself is stifled.

We have been wrong. We must change our lives, so that it will be possible to live by the contrary assumption that what is good for the world will be good for us. And that requires that we make the effort to *know* the world and to learn what is good for it. We must learn to cooperate in its processes, and to yield to its limits. But even more important, we must learn to acknowledge that the creation is full of mystery; we will never entirely understand it. We must abandon arrogance and stand in awe. We must recover the sense of the majesty of creation, and the ability to be worshipful in its presence. For I do not doubt that it is only on the condition of humility and reverence before the world that our species will be able to remain in it.

Standing in the presence of these worn and abandoned fields, where the creation has begun its healing without the hindrance or the help of man, with the voice of the stream in the air and the woods standing in silence on all the slopes around me, I am deep in the interior not only of my place in the world, but of my own life, its sources and searches and concerns. I first came into these places following the men to work when I was a child. I knew the men who took their lives from such fields as these, and their lives to a considerable extent made my life what it is. In what came to me from them there was both wealth and poverty, and I have been a long time discovering which was which.

It was in the woods here along Camp Branch that Bill White, my grandfather's Negro hired hand, taught me to hunt squirrels. Bill lived in a little tin-roofed house on up nearer the head of the hollow. And this was, I suppose more than any other place, his hunting ground. It was the place of his freedom, where he could move without subservience, without considering who he was or who anybody else was. On late summer mornings, when it was too wet to work, I would follow him into the woods. As soon as we stepped in under the trees he would become silent and absolutely attentive to the life of the place. He was a good teacher and an exacting one. The rule seemed to be that if I wanted to stay with him, I had to make it possible for him to forget I was there. I was to make no noise. If I did he would look back and make a downward emphatic gesture with his hand, as explicit as writing: Be quiet, or go home. He would see a squirrel crouched in a fork or lying along the top of a branch, and indicate with a grin and a small jerk of his head where I should look; and then wait, while I, conscious of being watched and demanded upon, searched it out for myself. He taught me to look and to listen and to be quiet. I wonder if he knew the value of such teaching or the rarity of such a teacher.

In the years that followed I hunted often here alone. And later in these same woods I experienced my first obscure dissatisfactions with hunting. Though I could not have put it into words then, the sense had come to me that hunting as I knew it – the eagerness to kill something I did not need to eat – was an artificial relation to the place, when what I was beginning to need, just as inarticulately then, was a relation that would be necessary and meaningful. That was a time of great uneasiness and restlessness for me. It would be the fall of the year, the leaves would be turning, and ahead of me would be another year of school. There would be confusions about girls and ambitions, the wordless hurried feeling that time and events and my own nature were pushing me toward what I was going to be – and I had no notion what it was, or how to prepare.

And then there were years when I did not come here at all – when these places and their history were in my mind, and part of me, in places thousands of miles away. And now I am here again, changed from what I was, and still changing. The future is no more certain to me now than it ever was, though its risks are clearer, and so are my own desires: I am the father of two young children whose lives are hostages given to the future. Because of them and because of events in the world, life seems more fearful and difficult to me now than ever before. But it is also more inviting, and I am constantly aware of its nearness to joy. Much of the interest and excitement that I have in my life now has come from the deepening, in the years since my return here, of my relation to this place. For in spite of all that has happened to me in other places, the great change and the great possibility of change in my life has been in my sense of this place. The major difference is perhaps only that I have grown able to be wholeheartedly present here. I am able to sit and be quiet at the foot of some tree here in this woods along Camp Branch, and feel a deep peace, both in the place and in my awareness of it, that not too long ago I was not conscious of the possibility of. This peace is partly in being free of the suspicion that pursued me for most of my life, no matter where I was, that there was perhaps another place I *should* be, or would be happier or better in; it is partly in the increasingly articulate consciousness of being here, and of the significance and importance of being here.

After more than thirty years I have at last arrived at the candor necessary to stand on this part of the earth that is so full of my own history and so much damaged by it, and ask: What *is* this place? What is in it? What is its nature? How should men live in it? What must I do?

I have not found the answers, though I believe that in partial and fragmentary ways they have begun to come to me. But the questions are more important than their answers. In the final sense they *have* no answers. They are like the questions – they are perhaps the same questions – that were the discipline of Job. They are a part of the necessary enactment of humility, teaching a man what his importance is, what his responsibility is, and what his place is, both on the earth and in the order of things. And though the answers must always come obscurely and in fragments, the questions must be asked. They are fertile questions. In their implications and effects, they are moral and aesthetic and, in the best and fullest sense, practical. They promise a relationship to the world that is decent and preserving.

They are also, both in origin and effect, religious. I am uneasy with the term, for such religion as has been openly practiced in this part of the world has promoted and fed upon a destructive schism between body and soul, Heaven and earth. It has encouraged people to believe that the world is of no importance, and that their only obligation in it is to submit to certain churchly formulas in order to get to Heaven. And so the people who might have been expected to care most selflessly for the world have had their minds turned elsewhere – to a pursuit of 'salvation' that was really only another form of gluttony and self-love, the desire to perpetuate their lives beyond the life of the world. The Heaven-bent have abused the earth thoughtlessly, by inattention, and their negligence has permitted and encouraged others to abuse it deliberately. Once the creator was removed from the creation, divinity became only a remote abstraction, a social weapon in the hands of the religious institutions. This split in public values produced or was accompanied by, as it was bound to be, an equally artificial and ugly division in people's lives, so that a man, while pursuing Heaven with the sublime appetite he thought of as his soul, could turn his heart against his neighbors and his hands against the world. For these reasons, though I know that my questions *are* religious, I dislike having to *say* that they are.

But when I ask them my aim is not primarily to get to Heaven. Though Heaven is certainly more important than the earth if all they say about it is true, it is still morally incidental to it and dependent on it, and I can only imagine it and desire it in terms of what I know of the earth. And so my questions do not aspire beyond the earth. They aspire *toward* it and *into* it. Perhaps they aspire *through* it. They are religious because they are asked at the limit of what I know; they acknowledge mystery and honor its presence in the creation; they are spoken in reverence for the order and grace that I see, and that I trust beyond my power to see.

The stream has led me down to an old barn built deep in the hollow to house the tobacco once grown on those abandoned fields. Now it is surrounded by the trees that have come back on every side – a relic, a fragment of another time, strayed out of its meaning. This is the last of my historical landmarks. To here, my walk has had insistent overtones of memory and history. It has been a movement of consciousness through knowledge, eroding and shaping, adding and wearing away. I have descended like the water of the stream through what I know of myself, and now that I have there is a little more to know. But here at the barn, the old roads and the cow paths – the formal connections with civilization – come to an end.

I stoop between the strands of a barbed-wire fence, and in that movement I go out of time into timelessness. I come into a wild place. The trees grow big, their trunks rising clean, free of undergrowth. The place has a serenity and dignity that one feels immediately; the creation is whole in it and unobstructed. It is free of the strivings and dissatisfactions, the partialities and imperfections of places under the mechanical dominance of men. Here, what to a house-keeper's eye might seem disorderly is none-theless orderly and within order; what might seem arbitrary or accidental is included in the design of the whole; what might seem evil or violent is a comfortable member of the household. Where the creation is whole nothing is extraneous. The presence of the creation here makes this a holy place, and it is as a pilgrim that I have come. It is the creation that has attracted me, its perfect interfusion of life and design. I have made myself its follower and its apprentice.

One early morning last spring, I came and found the woods floor strewn with bluebells. In the cool sunlight and the lacy shadows of the spring woods the blueness of those flowers, their elegant shape, their delicate fresh scent kept me standing and looking. I found a delight in them that I cannot describe and that I will never forget.

Though I had been familiar for years with most of the spring woods flowers, I had never seen these and had not known they were here. Looking at them, I felt a strange loss and sorrow that I had never seen them before. But I was also exultant that I saw them now – that they were here.

For me, in the thought of them will always be the sense of the joyful surprise with which I found them – the sense that came suddenly to me then that the world is blessed beyond my understanding, more abundantly than I will ever know. What lives are still ahead of me here to be discovered and exulted in, tomorrow, or in twenty years? What wonder will be found here on the morning after my death? Though as a man I inherit great evils and the possibility of great loss and suffering, I know that my life is blessed and graced by the yearly flowering of the bluebells. How perfect they are!

In their presence I am humble and joyful. If I were given all the learning and all the methods of my race I could not make one of them, or even imagine one. Solomon in all his glory was not arrayed like one of these. It is the privilege and the labor of the apprentice of creation to come with his imagination into the unimaginable, and with his speech into the unspeakable.

3

SOMETIMES I CAN no longer think in the house or in the garden or in the cleared fields. They bear too much resemblance to our failed human history – failed, because it has led to this human present that is such a bitterness and a trial. And so I go to the woods. As I go in under the trees, dependably, almost at once, and by nothing I do, things fall into place. I enter an order that does not exist outside, in the human spaces.

I feel my life take its place among the lives – the trees, the annual plants, the animals and birds, the living of all these and the dead – that go and have gone to make the life of the earth. I am less important than I thought, the human race is less important than I thought. I rejoice in that. My mind loses its urgings, senses its nature, and is free. The forest grew here in its own time, and so I will live, suffer and rejoice, and die in my own time. There is nothing that I may decently hope for that I cannot reach by patience as well as by anxiety. The hill, which is a part of America, has killed no one in the service of the American government. Then why should I, who am a fragment of the hill? I wish to be as peaceable as my land, which does no violence, though it has been the scene of violence and has had violence done to it.

How, having a consciousness, an

intelligence, a human spirit – all the vaunted equipment of my race – can I humble myself before a mere piece of the earth and speak of myself as its fragment? Because my mind transcends the hill only to be filled with it, to comprehend it a little, to know that it lives on the hill in time as well as in place, to recognize itself as the hill's fragment.

The false and truly belittling transcendence is ownership. The hill has had more owners than its owners have had years – they are grist for its mill. It has had few friends. But I wish to be its friend, for I think it serves its friends well. It tells them they are fragments of its life. In its life they transcend their years.

THE MOST EXEMPLARY nature is that of the topsoil. It is very Christ-like in its passivity and beneficence, and in the penetrating energy that issues out of its peaceableness.

It increases by experience, by the passage of seasons over it, growth rising out of it and returning to it, not by ambition or aggressiveness. It is enriched by all things that die and enter into it. It keeps the past, not as history or as memory, but as richness, new possibility. Its fertility is always building up out of death into promise. Death is the bridge or the tunnel by which its past enters its future.

TO WALK IN the woods, mindful only of the *physical* extent of it, is to go perhaps as owner, or as knower, confident of one's own history and of one's own importance. But to go there, mindful as well of its temporal extent, of the age of it, and of all that led up to the present life of it, and of all that may follow it, is to feel oneself a flea in the pelt of a great living thing, the discrepancy between its life and one's own so great that it cannot be imagined. One has come into the presence of mystery. After all the trouble one has taken to be a modern man, one has come back under the spell of a primitive awe, wordless and humble.

IN THE CENTURIES before its settlement by white men, among the most characteristic and pleasing features of the floor of this valley, and of the stream banks on its slopes, were the forests and the groves of great beech trees. With their silver bark and their light graceful foliage, turning gold in the fall, they were surely as lovely as any forests that ever grew on earth. I think so because I have seen their diminished descendants, which have returned to stand in the wasted places that we have so quickly misused and given up. But those old forests are all gone. We will never know them as they were. We have driven them beyond the reach of our minds, only a vague hint of their presence returning to haunt us, as though in dreams – a fugitive rumor of the nobility and beauty and abundance of the squandered maidenhood of our world – so that, do what we will, we will never quite be satisfied ever again to be here.

The country, as we have made it by the pretense that we can do without it as soon as we have completed its metamorphosis into cash, no longer holds even the possibility of such forests, for the topsoil that they made and stood upon, like children piling up and trampling underfoot the fallen leaves, is no longer here.

There is an ominous – perhaps a fatal – presumptuousness in living in a place by the *imposition* on it of one's ideas and wishes. And that is the way we white people have lived in America throughout our history, and it is the way our history now teaches us to live here.

Surely there could be a more indigenous life than we have. There could be a consciousness that would establish itself on a place by understanding its nature and learning what is potential in it. A man ought to study the wilderness of a place before applying to it the ways he learned in another place. Thousands of acres of hill land, here and in the rest of the country, were wasted by a system of agriculture that was fundamentally alien to it. For more than a century, here, the steepest hillsides were farmed, by my forefathers and their neighbors, as if they were flat, and as if this was not a country of heavy rains. We haven't yet, in any meaningful sense, arrived in these places that we declare we own. We undertook the privilege of the virgin abundance of this land without any awareness at all that we undertook at the same time a responsibility toward it. That responsibility has never yet impressed itself upon our character; its absence in us is signified on the land by scars.

Until we understand what the land is, we are at odds with everything we touch. And to come to that understanding it is necessary, even now, to leave the regions of our conquest – the cleared fields, the towns and cities, the highways – and reenter the woods. For only there can a man encounter the silence and the darkness of his own absence. Only in this silence and darkness can he recover the sense of the world's longevity, of its ability to thrive without him, of his inferiority to it and his dependence on it. Perhaps then, having heard that silence and seen that darkness, he will grow humble before the place and begin to take it in – to learn *from it* what it is. As its sounds come into his hearing, and its lights and colors come into his vision, and its odors come into his nostrils, then he may come into *its* presence as he never has before, and he will arrive in his place and will want to remain. His life will grow out of the ground like the other lives of the place, and take its place among them. He will be *with* them – neither ignorant of them, nor indifferent to them, nor against them – and so at last he will grow to be native-born. That is, he must re-enter the silence and the darkness, and be born again.

One winter night nearly twenty years ago I was in the woods with the coon hunters, and we were walking toward the dogs, who had moved out to the point of the bluff where the valley of Cane Run enters the valley of the river. The footing was difficult, and one of the hunters was having trouble with his lantern. The flame would 'run up' and smoke the globe, so that the light it gave obscured more than it illuminated, an obstacle between his eyes and the path. At last he cursed it and flung it down into a hollow. Its little light went looping down through the trees and disappeared, and there was a distant tinkle of glass as the globe shattered. After that he saw better and went along the bluff easier than before, and lighter, too.

Not long ago, walking up there, I came across his old lantern lying rusted in the crease of the hill, half buried already in the siftings of the slope, and I let it lie. But I've kept the memory that it renewed. I have made it one of my myths of the hill. It has come to be truer to me now than it was then.

For I have turned aside from much that I knew, and have given up much that went before. What will not bring me, more certainly than before, to where I am is of no use to me. I have stepped out of the clearing into the woods. I have thrown away my lantern, and I can see the dark.

THE HILL, LIKE Valéry's sycamore, is a voyager standing still. Never moving a step, it travels through years, seasons, weathers, days and nights. These are the measures of its time, and they alter it, marking their passage on it as on a man's face. The hill has never observed a Christmas or an Easter or a Fourth of July. It has nothing to do with a dial or a calendar. Time is told in it mutely and immediately, with perfect accuracy, as it is told by the heart in the body. Its time is the birth and the flourishing and the death of the many lives that are its life.

THE HILL IS like an old woman, all her human obligations met, who sits at work day after day, in a kind of rapt leisure, at an intricate embroidery. She has time for all things. Because she does not expect ever to be finished, she is endlessly patient with details. She perfects flower and leaf, feather and song, adorning the briefest life in great beauty as though it were meant to last forever.

IN THE EARLY spring I climb up through the woods to an east-facing bluff where the bloodroot bloom in scattered colonies around the foot of the rotting monument of a tree trunk. The sunlight is slanting, clear, through the leafless branches. The flowers are white and perfect, delicate as though shaped in air and water. There is a fragility about them that communicates how short a time they will last. There is some subtle bond between them and the dwindling great trunk of the dead tree. There comes on me a pressing wish to preserve them. But I know that what draws me to them would not pass over into anything I can *do*. They will be lost. In a few days none will be here.

COMING UPON A mushroom growing out of a pad of green moss between the thick roots of an oak, the sun and the dew still there together, I have felt my mind irresistibly become small, to inhabit that place, leaving me standing vacant and bewildered, like a boy whose captured field mouse has just leaped out of his hand.

AS I SLOWLY fill with the knowledge of this place, and sink into it, I come to the sense that my life here is inexhaustible, that its possibilities lie rich behind and ahead of me, that when I am dead it will not be used up.

TOO MUCH THAT we do is done at the expense of something else, or somebody else.

There is some intransigent destructiveness in us. My days, though I think I know better, are filled with a thousand irritations, worries, regrets for what has happened and fears for what may, trivial duties, meaningless torments – as destructive of my life as if I wanted to be dead. Take today for what it is, I counsel myself. Let it be enough.

And I dare not, for fear that if I do, yesterday will infect tomorrow. We are in the habit of contention – against the world, against each other, against ourselves.

It is not from ourselves that we will learn to be better than we are.

IN SPITE OF all the talk about the law of tooth and fang and the struggle for survival, there is in the lives of the animals and birds a great peacefulness. It is not all fear and flight, pursuit and killing. That is part of it, certainly; and there is cold and hunger;

there is the likelihood that death, when it comes, will be violent. But there is peace, too, and I think that the intervals of peace are frequent and prolonged. These are the times when the creature rests, communes with himself or with his kind, takes pleasure in being alive.

This morning while I wrote I was aware of a fox squirrel hunched in the sunlight on a high elm branch beyond my window. The night had been frosty, and now the warmth returned. He stayed there a long time, warming and grooming himself. Was he not at peace? Was his life not pleasant to him then?

I have seen the same peacefulness in a flock of wood ducks perched above the water in the branches of a fallen beech, preening and dozing in the sunlight of an autumn afternoon. Even while they dozed they had about them the exquisite alertness of wild things. If I had shown myself they would have been instantly in the air. But for the time there was no alarm among them, and no fear. The moment was whole in itself, satisfying to them and to me.

Or the sense of it may come with watching a flock of cedar waxwings eating wild grapes in the top of the woods on a November afternoon. Everything they do is leisurely. They pick the grapes with a curious deliberation, comb their feathers, converse in high windy whistles. Now and then one will fly out and back in a sort of dancing flight full of whimsical flutters and turns. They are like farmers loafing in their own fields on Sunday. Though they have no Sundays, their days are full of sabbaths.

ONE CLEAR FINE morning in early May, when the river was flooded, my friend and I came upon four rough-winged swallows circling over the water, which was still covered with frail wisps and threads of mist from the cool night. They were bathing, dipping down to the water until they touched the still surface with a little splash. They wound their flight over the water like the graceful falling loops of a fine cord. Later they perched on a dead willow, low to the water, to dry and groom themselves, the four together. We paddled the canoe almost within reach of them before they flew. They were neat, beautiful, gentle birds. Sitting there preening in the sun after their cold bath, they communicated a sense of domestic integrity, the serenity of living within order. We didn't belong within the order of the events and needs of their day, and so they didn't notice us until they had to.

BUT THERE IS not only peacefulness, there is joy. And the joy, less deniable in its

evidence than the peacefulness, is the con-
firmation of it. I sat one summer evening
and watched a great blue heron make his
descent from the top of the hill into the valley. He came down at a measured deliberate pace, stately as always, like a dignitary
going down a stair. And then, at a point I
judged to be midway over the river, without
at all varying his wingbeat he did a back-
ward turn in the air, a loop-the-loop. It
could only have been a gesture of pure exuberance, of joy – a speaking of his sense of
the evening, the day's fulfillment, his descent
homeward. He made just the one slow turn,
and then flew on out of sight in the direc-
tion of a slew farther down in the bottom.
The movement was incredibly beautiful, at
once exultant and stately, a benediction on
the evening and on the river and on me. It
seemed so perfectly to confirm the presence
of a free nonhuman joy in the world – a joy I

feel a great need to believe in – that I had the skeptic's impulse to doubt that I had seen it. If I had, I thought, it would be a sign of the presence of something heavenly in the earth. And then, one evening a year later, I saw it again.

EVERY MAN IS followed by a shadow which is his death – dark, featureless, and mute. And for every man there is a place where his shadow is clarified and is made his reflection, where his face is mirrored in the ground. He sees his source and his destiny, and they are acceptable to him. He becomes the follower of what pursued him. What hounded his track becomes his companion.

That is the myth of my search and my return.

I HAVE BEEN walking in the woods, and have lain down on the ground to rest. It is the middle of October, and around me, all through the woods, the leaves are quietly sifting down. The newly fallen leaves make a dry, comfortable bed, and I lie easy, coming to rest within myself as I seem to do nowadays only when I am in the woods.

And now a leaf, spiraling down in wild flight, lands on my shirt at about the third button below the collar. At first I am bemused and mystified by the coincidence – that the leaf should have been so hung, weighted and shaped, so ready to fall, so nudged loose and slanted by the breeze, as to fall where I, by the same delicacy of circumstance, happened to be lying. The event, among all its ramifying causes and considerations, and finally its mysteries, begins to take on the magnitude of history. Portent begins to dwell in it.

And suddenly I apprehend in it the dark proposal of the ground. Under the fallen leaf my breastbone burns with imminent decay. Other leaves fall. My body begins its long shudder into humus. I feel my substance escape me, carried into the mold by beetles and worms. Days, winds, seasons pass over me as I sink under the leaves. For a time only sight is left me, a passive awareness of the sky overhead, birds crossing, the mazed interreaching of the treetops, the leaves falling – and then that, too, sinks away. It is acceptable to me, and I am at peace.

When I move to go, it is as though I rise up out of the world.

(1968)